KT-555-892

An interview with

Theresa Breslin

by Lindsey Fraser

mammoth

Other authors in the *Telling Tales* series:
Gillian Cross, Anne Fine, Michelle Magorian,
Michael Morpurgo, Jenny Nimmo

Lindsey Fraser is a leading children's book
enthusiast. She started work in James Thin Booksellers
in Edinburgh, before managing Heffers Children's
Bookshop in Cambridge. She is now Executive Director
of Scottish Book Trust, an organisation renowned for its
work in promoting reading amongst children and in
raising the profile of children's literature.

Published in Great Britain 1999 by Mammoth, an imprint of Egmont Children's
Books Limited, 239 Kensington High Street, London W8 6SA.

Interview questions, design and typesetting © 1999 Egmont Children's Books
Interview answers © 1999 Theresa Breslin
Theresa's Books © 1999 Lindsey Fraser

ISBN 0 7497 3867 7

A CIP catalogue record for this title is available from the British Library.

Printed and bound in Great Britain
by Cox & Wyman Ltd, Reading, Berks.

Contents

An interview with Theresa Breslin
by Lindsey Fraser

Theresa's Books

Theresa Breslin is a writer and librarian with a special interest in children's literature, whose first book won Scottish Book Trust's Fidler Award for new writers. She has been described as an outstanding writer, who creates memorable characters, combining a powerful sense of drama with superb storytelling. Her books appear regularly on children's book award shortlists, are in translation in a number of languages, and have been dramatised on television and radio. *Death or Glory Boys* won the longer novel category of the Sheffield Book Award, *Kezzie* was shortlisted for the Children's Book Award, and *Whispers in the Graveyard* won the Carnegie Gold Medal, the UK's most prestigious children's book award.

An interview with
Theresa Breslin
by Lindsey Fraser

My family and my childhood

What did your family consist of?

There were six children: five girls and one boy. I was the second youngest. My dad was the school janitor – the 'jannie' – and we lived in the basement flat of a big house in the grounds of the school.

I really got on with everybody in the family, except for the usual arguments. I probably played more with the younger ones though, and we had cousins who came to visit a lot.

Were your grandparents important during your childhood?

I remember my father's mother as being a traditional wee

Theresa aged four, sitting on Grandad's knee.

granny in a black shawl, but we didn't see as much of her as of my mother's father. Grandad was a real character. He came to the house a lot and we would visit him in Kirkintilloch in his one room and kitchen, with its gas mantle – he never had electricity and he died in the late sixties. His door was never locked and he had a great birthday party every year. Everybody came. I remember he told a great story, embroidering the facts, always entertaining his friends. He had a very active life even when I knew him – he had time for everyone.

Did you have any animals?

The school had animals – lots of cats. And my brother had two budgies. We had white mice too – but not in the house!

Where were you born?

I was born in Kirkintilloch in the house where I grew up. It was a great house – huge rooms, every one with a fire-place. We were never short of hot water and the house was always warm because it was part of the school. When I was a teenager and my dad retired we moved to a coun-cil house in town and I really hated it. We had good neighbours, but it was never home. Of course the school house had lawns and gardens, great for cycling and roller-skating, although I also remember playing on the huge coal dumps which wasn't allowed at all! My dad grew masses of our food – potatoes and leeks – and he also grew grapes and tomatoes in a greenhouse. The council house was one in a long row of other

Theresa aged eleven (right)
in the gardens of the school.

houses just like it, with a tiny garden.

Kirkintilloch was a rural town with mines round about it. The problem in a small town is that everybody knows you. One thing I hated was shopping with my mother. She'd leave each one of us in a different shop with the list of messages – these were the days when you had to queue at a counter to be served – and then she'd come back just in time to pay. Everyone thought she was jumping the queue! Mostly I'd go to town to go to the library. I just loved going to the library.

Glasgow was the nearest big city. It was a real treat to take the bus to Glasgow. I remember we'd go to the Kelvin Hall to see the Christmas Carnival.

Do you have happy memories of childhood?

Yes. My parents were strict but I think we were happy. When I was a teenager I wasn't very biddable and there were lots of rows with my parents. I always felt I was missing out on something, but looking back – and having had children of my own – I understand a bit better why they were like they were. Although I still think they were a bit too strict at times.

The greatest thing about my childhood was the freedom . . . and books, of course.

I loved Christmas too, because my mother really pulled out all the stops. We didn't have a lot of money and there were few luxuries, so Christmas was a very special time. Midnight Mass was really,

Theresa's mother.

really exciting. When we came out it always felt colder! And in the morning, opening the presents – I remember a brilliant Post Office set. It had a stamp and I loved stamping things. Maybe that's why I became a librarian!

We went to Mass every Sunday and I enjoyed that. I loved the words, the rhythms and patterns of the language, the incense and the litanies. I never remember being forced to go. I liked the discipline of it – it felt important. My dad didn't just accept everything, he didn't go out of fear or servitude. I remember they used to have missions with special preachers where there were Women's Nights and Men's Nights and I was always desperate to go to the Men's Night to find out what went on!

My only really unhappy memories of childhood are nightmares. I hated the dark – although I'm quite happy to walk around outside in the dark – and had vivid nightmares. I still do, although sometimes they're just dreams and I occasionally wake with whole stories, dialogue and all.

But I was terribly upset when my Grandad died. It was awful. I was much younger when my Granny died and I quite enjoyed all the activity, coming and going, but not with my Grandad. We all missed him badly.

My schooldays

What was your first school like?

I really hated primary school. Or at least most of it. One good teacher was Miss Docherty. She didn't shout – she asked. She didn't threaten, and I remember she told stories. It probably helped that she was quite young. I won't give the name of my most hated teacher because she may still be alive, but she could be very nasty indeed. I thought she hated me particularly but then I discovered that everyone thought that she hated them. My dad was furious at some of the things she taught us; looking back she was quite anti-Scottish and he didn't like that. He'd recite *Lochinvar* to me when she was teaching us *Drake's Drum*!

I don't remember learning to read. My dad read to us, and my sisters did too, and there were always books around at home – lovely editions which must have cost my dad quite a lot. I've still got many of them, and books I won for prizes – *The Water Babies* and *The Little Folk Picture Book*.

What was your secondary school like?

I much preferred secondary school – St Ninian's High School. There was so much more freedom. By the time I was half way through, we had moved from the school grounds so I didn't have that constant 'I'll tell your father' going on. It meant I was able to go off the rails a bit! Not that I really did . . .

What was your favourite subject?

History and English. I liked European history but all the Scottish history and the Celtic legends I learned were from my dad. I got a prize for English I remember.

What was your most hated subject?

Maths, definitely. I couldn't do it, still can't. I just don't understand it. But I did like science. Latin was a problem. I worked out the way the vocabulary tests went round the class so I learned every sixth word, until I was caught out when somebody before me was off sick! After that I thought I'd better learn the fifth and the seventh words too.

Who was your favourite teacher?

My English teacher, Mr Kearns, was very inspirational. He took us to see plays at the Citizen's Theatre in Glasgow, and he'd act out the parts in class. He was great.

Who was your most hated teacher?

The funny thing is that I wasn't scared of any of the teachers in secondary school. They treated us more like human beings than in primary school where they used intimidation more, and verbal bullying.

What was your handwriting like then?

I had beautiful handwriting, believe it or not. I wrote in chancery script which is very slow to do.

... But words, words are different.
I heard poetry on the radio once.
The phrases stayed inside me for weeks,
exploding in my head, thrusting and
twisting in my gut.

An example of Theresa's chancery script handwriting.

Did your teachers think you might become a writer?

My English teacher was quite encouraging, but that
idea would have been considered far too pretentious in
primary school.

What are your first memories of reading?

I always remember seeing my dad read. He loved books.
My mother read but not so often – she must have been
incredibly busy. I joined the library when I was four and
a half.

Was reading important to you?

It was words that were important. I just remember that

words always meant a lot to me. I realised quite early that they were powerful. I was quite sensitive, I suppose, and very aware of how distraught words could make me. I probably got the belt once or twice, but much worse than that was teachers being sarcastic.

What kind of child were you?

I was quite quiet – I still am. I don't mind being on my own but I do like being in company. I love it when my children have friends round. I love sitting listening to them.

**Theresa aged eight (front left)
outside her aunt's house.**

Were friends more important than family?

With having such a big family, I think the family was more important.

Who was your favourite children's author?

All of them! Angela Brazil, Elinor Brent Dyer, Enid Blyton, Captain E. Johns. Really, I'd read whatever books I could lay my hands on!

Theresa aged ten (left) on the beach.

What was your favourite children's book then?

It's very hard to choose just one. I remember fairy tales illustrated by Arthur Rackham that terrified the wits out of me! My favourite children's book now is Mary Norton's *The Borrowers*. I came to it when I was older. It has such profound observations about life – like all really classic children's books – including 'What are human beans for?'

When did you start reading adult writers?

In Kirkintilloch Library they had Dickens' novels in the junior library. I remember reading *A Tale Of Two Cities* – the first book I ever read without a totally happy ending. It's got a great opening line and a great closing line. I remember I bought that book and I still think it's a brilliant book. I also read Sir Walter Scott, G.K. Chesterton, Hilaire Belloc and Maurice Walsh. My dad had all these other books at home too – *Lives of the Saints*, *Caesar's Conquest of Gaul*, *St John of the Cross* – some pretty heavy religious writing. I read everything.

Did you read poetry?

Yes, lots, especially ballads. My dad loved ballads.

Did you read non-fiction?

We had a subscription to the *National Geographic Magazine*. It made me want to travel. I remember cutting out bits about the Aswan Dam. My parents read lots of biographies, so I read them too.

What music did you listen to?

My sisters and aunts played the piano and the organ so I heard quite a lot of that! I remember listening to Radio Luxembourg too. I can't work with background noise – I like silence. If I'm listening to music I like film music, or popular classics. I went to a Bob Dylan concert recently which was brilliant! And I like Leonard Cohen and Edith Piaff.

Do you like looking at paintings?

Yes, I love it. I visit galleries wherever I go; there are stories in paintings and I like asking myself what happened just before, or just afterwards. I especially like the Pre-Raphaelites and the Impressionists.

What part did cinema, drama and TV play in your childhood?

TV played almost no part, but I did like the cinema.

What part do they play now?

TV's not very important, although there are things I enjoy very much indeed. *Blackadder* I loved, especially the series set during World War I. It's true comedy but so sad. I still enjoy the cinema – although I'm quite squeamish – but I'm most affected by theatre.

Do you have a favourite actor or actress?

Probably Daniel Day Lewis, in *The Last of the Mohicans*. It's very violent – but I watch it on video with the fast forward to hand!

What TV do you watch now?

Star Trek. It's interesting to see how they use story lines from classical Greek myths.

What was your favourite film?

Ben Hur was unbelievable! And *The Ten Commandments*. Big epics.

Do you have a favourite film now?

The Last of the Mohicans, of course. And *Cinema Paradiso* – I'd want to watch them both again. I thought DiCaprio was quite good in *Romeo and Juliet*.

My career

After you left school, what did you do?

My father wanted me to be a teacher – so I decided to become a librarian! He was determined that his daughters would have professions. Some people thought he was quite ambitious for us but he just had a vision for us, for our future.

After I left school I went to work in the Mitchell Library in Glasgow and then, because I realised I'd need qualifications to get on, I went to study librarianship in Birmingham. I came back to work in Glasgow District branch libraries.

By that time I was married and when we started a family I gave up my job. I was away from librarianship for eight years, until the children went to school. Then I joined East Dunbartonshire Library Service. I became a librarian on board the mobile library, then a community librarian and until recently a youth services librarian.

My career as a writer

Did you write as a child?

I do remember trying to write, but I didn't feel it was

encouraged in primary school to the extent that it is now.

My sisters and I did write plays though, often of a religious nature, and performed them to long-suffering aunts and uncles. I was a trouble-maker – I knew that if I really screamed I'd get what I wanted! I remember once when we were doing the Nativity Story, I was one of the three kings and I saw my sister with two crowns. I started a real temper tantrum, thinking I wouldn't have a crown, so she gave me one to shut me up. Then I realised that the person without the crown would have their face all made up! I was furious but I had the crown so I couldn't complain. Of course my sister knew exactly what was what . . .

How did you become a published writer?

I'd always had it in the back of my mind that I might write a book, but I really started to work at my writing when I went to the local writers' group – The Strathkelvin Writers' Group – with my sister. The writer Margaret Thomson Davies gave us exercises and one time she read mine aloud and said, 'This is a writer.' I was dead chuffed. At the time I was working around Gartcosh, and was very aware of the effects of the closure of the steel mills. I wrote about that and everybody in the group said, 'Get that finished. Go on, and get it finished.' So I did, and I sent it off to the Kathleen Fidler Prize – a great prize for a first novel for children – and I won it! Then I knew I could do it and it just made me want to do it again.

Theresa winning the Fidler Award for *Simon's Challenge*.

Do you like being a writer?

Yes – but it has its downside. You need confidence to work on your own. Recently I stopped working as a librarian and I miss the company. I miss the books too, and talking about the books. When you work on your own you lose objectivity – you begin laughing at your own jokes! It helps when I go out and about – talking with parents and children about books. I never mind talking about other people's books either.

What do you like best about writing?

I like it when it works. You can do what you like with your own imagination, and I feel good – physically and mentally – when I sit down to write. And I love it when the finished book comes in, and seeing copies in shops. I'm quite a child when it comes to that.

Are there things you don't like about being a writer?

When it doesn't work! Also it can be very lonely, especially when your ideas don't gel and when I know what I want to say but I just can't say it.

Is writing an obsession or a compulsion?

It's a compulsion but definitely not an obsession. In a way, though, I'm working all the time because I'm always listening for stories. I'm nosy. I find people interesting. I remember hearing the start of what I knew was going to be a fascinating story in a café in Canada. Well, I said I was nosy! My husband was all set to get up and go – we'd finished our drink. I couldn't believe it! I said to him, 'How can you not want to know what happened? How can you just walk away?' He knows me well so we sat back down and heard it all. And it was a brilliant story. All sorts of possibilities . . .

Have you changed the way you write?

I've certainly learned a lot. I can spot mistakes in other people's books – although not necessarily in my own.

How long does it take you to write a book?

A longer novel – *Whispers in the Graveyard* or *Death or Glory Boys* – will take a year. And it can be very exhausting. Of that year, the writing will probably take four to six months. A shorter story – *Blair the Winner* or *Name*

Games – might take about six weeks to three months. But there's always a lot of thinking before I start the writing. And I think I'm quite a slow writer.

Is there a pattern to the writing day?

I won't sit down to write unless I've got a minimum of three hours ahead without interruption. It's hard because I'm involved in so many things, but I am quite disciplined. I used to write from nine in the evening until midnight. Except sometimes I'd look up and it would be three in the morning. The night-time's a good time for me to write.

How do you write?

After I've done all the research I think I'm going to need, and gathered all my notes together on bits of paper, I put the story down quite quickly, but very roughly on the computer. I don't write consecutively. I know that sounds weird but it's true. I write in scenes really, and my notes remind me of the things I need my reader to know. The trouble with a computer over a pencil and paper is that when you delete, you have no reminder of what you put originally. So I probably have four drafts printed from my computer before I'm ready to hand it over.

I value a good, gentle editor because, like most writers, I've got a fragile ego. The editor's opinion is so important. I don't like to let anyone read it before I've given it to the editor, although occasionally I've let somebody in the family read it.

Do you listen to criticism?

Oh yes. You've got to. But I was gratified to hear P.D. James talk about her insecurities when she sends in her manuscript to the publisher, phoning her editor at two-hourly intervals to find out how she likes it! It's not easy to hand over your book.

Why do you write for children?

I didn't automatically write for children. The first story I ever wrote – it's never been published and if you read it you'd know why – was like an extension of the exercises we were set in the writers' group. I don't know why, I just started writing and the character I was writing about was a child. I don't think it's necessary to be exclusive. Children's books are universal. A good children's book can be read satisfactorily by adults. I think writing for children is more interesting – there's far more scope.

Where do your ideas come from?

Everywhere – life, people, incidents. And my imagination. Everything I write is inspired by a real incident. I never have to look for ideas, they stick themselves under my nose! My problem is that I have far too many ideas, boxes of notes, wee cuttings out of the newspapers. When you write you discipline your ideas. That's the hard thing.

What subjects appeal to you?

There isn't a subject that doesn't appeal. I was surprised that I enjoyed writing *Alien Force*, a science fiction novel, so much, but it gave free rein to my imagination. I didn't have to worry about the rules of real life, and you can't ignore them if you're writing about the real world. It's fine to be running around on your own in the middle of the night on the Planet Zarg, but not down the middle of Sauchiehall Street. Your parents would be frantic with worry!

What kind of research do you do?

I love research. I really love it. Sometimes it's a trial to begin to write the book. I love looking through news-papers, maps and letters – letters are particularly good. I also love handling objects – a miner's lamp, his kneepads. It's like gardening. You can listen to all the gardening programmes you like but until you've got earth under your fingernails you really don't know anything. I also love talking to people. You can talk about the war, but if you talk to somebody who was *in* the war the difference is incredible.

How important is imagination?

Vital. Stories pivot on the imagination – the writer's imagination and the reader's imagination. That's one of the great mysteries about books. Sometimes a reader will point out a part they've loved in one of your books and you'll be quite surprised. And then of course they'll have skipped the bit you spent days getting right!

How do events in your life or your family's life affect your stories?

All my books start with real incidents. The family definitely feeds into the books but I don't rely on them. The scene at the beginning of *Death or Glory Boys* – the shoe shopping trip – is certainly true to life. Children are constantly inventing new ways to torture their parents and shopping is one of them! But young people can laugh at themselves, they bond with situations they recognise.

Do you base your characters on real people?

On strands of real people. Phil in *Death or Glory Boys* really reflects my opinions, I suppose. Kezzie was based on my wee auntie. She lived in a mining village and she was always telling us how great it was. We just didn't believe it and when I did my historical research it was incredible – girls in their early teens with responsibility for entire families because their mothers had died. My own mother's elder sister did that when their mother died. The men were out at work so they just had to get on with it. I wanted to write a story about that but I knew I'd need more of a plot for it.

What matters most to you – the story or the characters?

I don't think you can divide the two. They grow out of each other and into each other.

Whom do you write for?

I write for the story. They say that Michaelangelo spent a year looking for the right piece of marble for a sculpture – he said that then he only had to chip away the bits that shouldn't be there. Writing stories is a bit like that. It's very exciting.

Which of your books is your favourite?

That depends on the mood I'm in. I like the funny ones but if they were the only books I'd written it wouldn't be very satisfying. I love wee children. Those funny books – *Name Games* and *Blair the Winner* – are truthful to them and I love working with that age group. But then I'll be talking to adults and kids with real problems and they'll tell me how much they've gained from reading *Whispers in the Graveyard*, how they go back to it again and again. That can be extraordinary. Then I love Solomon.

Which is your favourite character in your own books?

I don't know. I like them all, even the bad ones. They've always got a good reason for behaving badly. And it's the bad characters who make the books. They throw up the challenge for the hero to overcome.

Are pictures important in your books?

I've been lucky with my illustrators. In *Body Parts*, a graphic novel, I had to write in a different way. It took a while to get the hang of it. I ended up writing the story twice, first for the story and then for illustration. The description became absorbed in the pictures and the dialogue went into speech bubbles. It was very interesting to do. I'd love to do a picture story book but they are very, very difficult, a bit like writing a poem.

What gives you most satisfaction about being a writer?

A sense of completion.

What do you dislike most about being a writer?

Isolation and self-doubt.

What do you hope to achieve with your books?

I want my readers to enjoy a good story and . . . anything else they can get out of it. Stories should expand and extend our own humanity, and they can do that in addition to being entertaining.

Why are books important?

I think they're more accessible than any other form of communication. They engage us on a much deeper level.

Why is fiction important?

Fiction can help you make sense out of life. It keeps you in touch with the emotional and the thinking part of your brain. It helps you understand.

Will it still be important in the new century?

Definitely.

Do you think TV can complement reading?

I think TV can stimulate reading. As a librarian I remember books lying on the shelf until they were adapted for television and then the issue figures would go through the roof. *Anne of Green Gables*, *The Last of the Mohicans*, *The Borrowers* – it happens all the time.

Which book has influenced your life?

How can I pick just one? I suppose it would have to be the Bible because I was used to hearing it and reading it every week and – hopefully at least – living it every week. But we had so many books. Celtic folk tales. Hilaire Belloc's *Cautionary Tales*. *The Arabian Nights* – I remember this old, ancient, big, thick book with its magnificent, scary illustrations. I mean, they chopped their heads off – there was no messing about! And poetry – poetry matters a great deal.

Which book comforts you most?

Poetry books. If I can't sleep, or I'm not feeling so good, I'll read poetry.

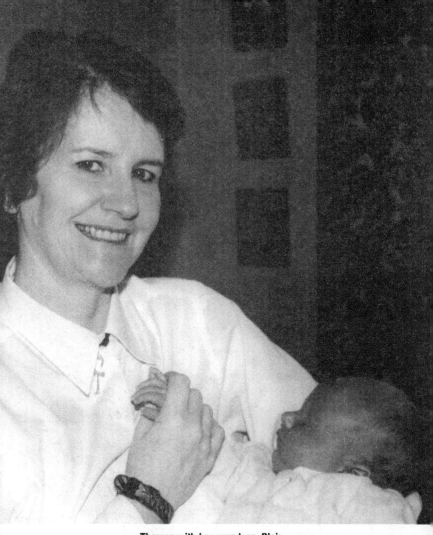
Theresa with her grandson, Blair.

Illustration by Ken Cox from *Blair the Winner!*

Theresa's Books
An overview by Lindsey Fraser

THERESA BRESLIN has read books all her life. She has a passion for books, and as a librarian, has shared that passion with people of all ages. Like many people, she always knew that she wanted to write a book, but unlike many people, Theresa succeeded. Now an established writer with an international reputation, Theresa has made a huge impact on those who read her stories, and she continues to enthuse young readers about reading through her work as a librarian and during her many visits to schools and libraries.

If you go into a bookshop or a library, you'll find hundreds, perhaps thousands of books written and illustrated for young people. Every year new books are published, adding to those which have been eagerly read and re-read for decades. *Alice's Adventures in Wonderland* was published in 1865, *Winnie the Pooh* in 1926, Noddy was invented in 1949 – these books are still popular today with children whose parents and grandparents also read and enjoyed them.

Not all books have such long and successful lives, of course. For a book to remain in print it must, in some way, be a special book, and the likelihood is that the author who created that book will be a special author.

Simon's Challenge

Simon's Challenge

Theresa Breslin's first book, *Simon's Challenge*, was published in 1988. It was immediately singled out as a special book because it won the Kathleen Fidler Award. This prize is given to an unpublished first novel for readers aged between eight and twelve years and the judges clearly recognised great talent in Theresa's writing.

The challenge for Simon is to solve a mystery. He knows that he is the only person who can reveal the identity of thieves who have ransacked Mr Peterson's computer shop. But the information seems locked in his brain and it is only when his memory is jolted that it leaks out, bit by bit. *Simon's Challenge* is a clever detective story, but there is much more to it than that. Simon is not some great hero with broad shoulders and good looks; he is an ordinary boy with problems of his own. It was because he was so preoccupied with these that he failed to notice exactly what was happening at Mr Peterson's store as he walked home from his friend's house one evening.

Simon's life is full of confusion. While his father is away looking for work he stays at home with his mother and his baby sister, Jessica. He is very like lots of young people his age. He desperately wants a computer. He loves his little sister – and is a splendid big brother to her – but sometimes he wishes she didn't take up so much time and attention. He misses his father, but is annoyed by him at the same time. Why can't he be at home like any normal father? Why doesn't he come back? Why can't he find a job?

The problem of unemployment and its effect on children, families and small communities inspired Theresa to write that first novel. At the time she was the mobile librarian for Gartcosh, a town near Glasgow, which was shattered by the closure of the local steel works. She decided to write about how a child feels when a parent is made redundant. In her novel Simon's father, like many others in the fictional town of Glenburn, is unemployed. The local steel works have been closed – a disaster for the local community. It isn't simply a case of having to go 'on the dole'. Mr Ross has lost his confidence. Simon and his mother know that he's given up hope and that his search for work on the oil rigs up north is really a way of escaping his problems.

Simon's mother watched him from the kitchen window. She shook her head, and reached for a tea towel. That boy really needs his father back, she thought as she began to dry the dishes. It was nearly six months since Joe had been at home. Supposedly he was looking for work up North. She sighed, knowing that Joe was glad to get away from tensions created by little money and no prospects. Funny how they had stuck together through the struggle when there had been a glimmer of hope that the steel works might be saved. The fight had seemed to bond people together, united in one effort. Then came the awful realisation that it wasn't going to happen – there would be no reprieve. A life of school clothing grants and Social Security giros stretched ahead of them.

Of course there are other important people in Simon's life and he is fortunate in having a teacher who is sensitive to the impact unemployment can have. She takes a very determined stance when the announcement about the closure of the steel works is made.

'I know that you all have fathers, uncles, brothers or cousins who work there, and there is a difficult time ahead. The closure will affect this whole community drastically. Now I am not going to discuss the rights and wrongs of that decision, but there is one thing I would like to say. Simon, read out the definition of the word which is on the blackboard, please.'

'Redundant,' Simon read out, 'Surplus to requirements, unnecessary, or superfluous.'

'Thank you, Simon. Go and sit down.' Mrs Davies turned and pointed to the blackboard. 'This word and its meaning applies to things,' she said, 'not to our workers. Only things, that is machines, or the skill to operate them, can become redundant. The world may no longer have any use for the works or the steel it produces, but we always have use for human beings. People do not become superfluous. Not even

when they are little and helpless as a baby is. We always need each other. We, all of us, have something to give. It is very important indeed that you all understand this. People are never redundant.'

Sometimes in Theresa's books, one of the characters will say something very definite like that, something about which this author feels very strongly. Her books are all about the importance of the individual, often against considerable odds. Not only does Simon have to struggle to help catch the burglars, he also has to take on family responsibilities beyond his years until his father returns with plans for the future.

Whispers in the Graveyard

Solomon, in *Whispers in the Graveyard*, is less fortunate than Simon. His mother has left him alone with his father who is an alcoholic. His life is miserable. He hates school where he is despised and bullied by one of his teachers. The main problem is that he, like his father, cannot

Whispers in the Graveyard

read. Solomon is actually dyslexic, which means that when he looks at letters on a page, they can appear jumbled and don't make sense. He has difficulty writing too. But because he has been labelled as a trouble-maker and is disruptive in class, nobody has taken the trouble to find out the cause of his problems. He has, to all intents and purposes, been written off as a no-hoper.

My jotter is dangling from Watkins' fingers. He sneers as he reads it out. 'No saturbay I was a footdall maSh . . .' His face is pushed up against mine, cheese and oniony breath smells in my face. Crepey skin sags around his eyes, little red broken veins make crazed lines on the whites.

Don't stand so stand so stand so close to me.

'You are a lazy stupid boy.' Thump, thump, on the desk.

Whispers in the Graveyard is a tough novel, but because it concerned something about which the author was so passionate, it couldn't have been anything else. So determined was Theresa to find out how it feels to be dyslexic that for a fortnight she read the daily newspaper in the mirror. She says, 'At the end of five days I wanted to bang my head against the wall.' But how else could she have described what Solomon saw when he looked at words 'tremble and merge, swimming across the page'? She knew how appalling he felt and how isolated his inability to read left him and it would have been dishonest to dilute those feelings. She also knew, because of her research, that there were ways to help Solomon. But the most important thing for Solomon is to find somebody he can trust, so that he can start to work on his problems. It takes some time, but he does find that support.

Whispers in the Graveyard also has some very frightening moments, far more frightening than many horror novels. The graveyard, where Solomon goes to get away from things, is the source of a terrifying story in which Solomon becomes implicated, a story based on folklore going back to the sixteenth and seventeenth centuries. Graveyards play an important part in many of Theresa's books. She is fascinated by the information to be found in them. So is Solomon, because much of the information is written in symbols and not words.

Dyslexia is a very real problem and *Whispers in the Graveyard* has done much to help readers of all ages understand the difficulties that children like Solomon face.

Kezzie

Kezzie

Kezzie was inspired by the plight of British orphans who were shipped to Canada during the Depression of the 30s, often without any record being kept of their whereabouts. Of course, this would never happen in Britain today, but there are still people alive who were sent abroad and who have lived all their lives apart from their natural family. A series of disasters which begin with the death of Kezzie's father in a mining

accident, culminate in the disappearance of her
little sister, Lucy, sent to Canada by the authorities. Kezzie has no choice but to sail after her
and bring her home.

'Granddad, you know that I have to go. There is
no other way to be absolutely sure of bringing
her back. She will be terrified and she needs me
with her as quickly as possible.' Kezzie stopped,
her eyes brimming with tears. 'You also know,'
she went on, 'that it's best you stay here and keep
on your job, for us to have something to come
back to.'

The sequel, *A Homecoming for Kezzie*, is the
story of the girls' life in Glasgow during World
War II. Lucy's safe return doesn't mean that Kezzie
can relax, but she, like so many of Theresa's characters, learns the value of true friendship and
loyalty. War can have a strange effect on people
who normally live perfectly happily together. In
peace-time, the Italian family for whom Kezzie

works are popular members of the community, their café a welcome part of Clydebank life. Although people often come together in times of difficulty, war can breed distrust, suspicion and even hatred, as the Biagis discover when their café is attacked. It takes great strength of character to stand up for others in such difficult circumstances. But Kezzie loathes injustice and exposes the racism for the cowardly bullying it is.

Humour

Although many of Theresa's novels are about serious subjects, she has a very strong sense of humour. *Death or Glory Boys* is a tense thriller but begins with a hilarious episode in a shoe shop. Sarah has taken her friends Maggie, Phil and David to buy a pair of boots but – as people tend to in shoe shops – she becomes distracted by the range.

Death or Glory Boys

Phil came up behind her. 'Boots,' he said in her ear. 'Concentrate girl. Boots. Do you intend to buy boots today? Do you intend to buy boots at all?'

'Of course I intend to buy boots,' said Sarah. 'That's what we came into the shop for. Chunky boots.'

'May I enquire, then,' said Phil folding his arms, 'if you are on a mission to buy long chunky boots, why you are, in fact, at this very moment trying on a flat pink shoe?'

Theresa also uses her books to include a little self-promotion! In *New School Blues*, Mary, newly arrived at her secondary school, awaits the distribution of the class reader in the hope that it will tell her something about the others in her class.

New School Blues

I checked around me. Let's see who would be getting War *and* Peace *and who was stuck with* Topsy *and* Tim visit the Dentist.

They were all the same. Simon's Challenge *by Theresa Breslin, published by*

Canongate. I flicked through a few pages. It looked good.

Theresa also has great fun with families. They play an important part in her books because, whatever their shape or size, everybody's life is affected by the people with whom they live. She is an author who feels that it would be unrealistic for her characters to be running around having adventures with nobody worrying about what they were doing. But the grown-ups don't always get it right. In *Blair the Winner*, Blair's mother asks her husband to explain to their son why sharing is so important. He is a little hesitant to begin with but soon gets into his stride.

Blair the Winner

'Anyway,' said Blair's dad, 'I take you to the park and we share a game together, and I let you have a go with my best leather football, signed by the World Cup Squad.' Blair's dad nodded once or twice.

'So there you are, that's how it works. Sharing is better than not sharing. OK, son?' He leaned over and ruffled Blair's hair. 'OK?'

'No,' said Blair, 'that's not true. I hardly ever get the ball. You always kick it up high where I can't reach it. And you want to score all the goals, and I never get to win a game.'

Blair's dad's face went quite pink. He quickly lay back on the couch and closed his eyes.

'Really, Andy!' Blair's mum tutted. 'I'm surprised at you!'

Children and adults

Sometimes the adults in Theresa's books are not any more grown-up than their children. Solomon's dad, in *Whispers in the Graveyard*, certainly needs Solomon to look after him. Sometimes they are not to be trusted. In *Alien Force*, Theresa's science fiction novel, Jodie finds himself completely isolated when he realises that the very people he trusts are the people who are intent on destroying him.

Whispers in the Graveyard

Alien Force

In *Different Directions*, Katharine and her mother have other problems. Katharine is quietly proud of her mother because she has decided to go back to school to gain some qualifications. However it is Katharine's school that she is attending and, although her friends love her mother, Katharine has very mixed feelings about her being there. She is huffy and uncommunicative until she discovers that her mother is ill. Then the two of them have to learn to trust each other.

In *The Dream Master*, Cy's dreams transport him into an adventure in which the world of the pharaohs comes into direct conflict with his own modern-day world. Those dreams are supposed to be in the control of the all-powerful Dream Master but he has to contend with a dreamer determined to dream his own dreams. The resulting entertaining adventure is, again, about trusting people and finding ways to solve seemingly impossible situations.

The power of words

Words, as one would expect of a writer, are of vital importance to Theresa. But they are also important to many of her characters. In *Name Games*, Jane finds as many words as she can to express her disgust at her boring name.

Name Games

She had checked her English thesaurus. There were tons of words that fitted the situation. She had practised saying some of them aloud. If anyone ever asked her what she thought of her name, she would be ready.

'My name,' she would say, 'fills me with a deep and intense sense of disgust.'

In *Simon's Challenge*, Simon loves the names of the stars and constellations. Although he can't read properly, Solomon, in *Whispers in the Graveyard*, adores words, revelling in the stories he's heard. But Theresa is all too aware of the power of words and in Solomon's case, a single word has a terrifying effect on the troubled boy.

Simon's Challenge

Whispers in the Graveyard

MALEFICE.

The word uncurls out from the page and spits at me.

'What . . . what is that word?'

Professor Miller leans over my shoulder. 'It is a Scottish word for witchcraft, or the practice of evil.'

There is a deep dark shadow in the room.

Stretching out over the earth.

A lengthening darkness unfolding, slowly chilling the air.

An evil purpose spreading its deadly intent.

Now . . . I can see from the window, down into the street. Onto the stupid and puny humans scuttling about below me.

My breath hisses through my teeth. Through narrowed eyes I watch them. They have tried to grind me down, now I will crush them.

Bodyparts   In *Bodyparts*, a graphic novel, words and pictures blend to create a tense thriller. The look of this book is, of course, completely different from Theresa's other novels, but the words are just as carefully chosen to have exactly the desired effect on her readers.

So much to say

We have looked at just a few of Theresa's books here. But in this selection we can see what makes her a special writer. If you spread her books out in front of you, you will see such a wide variety of writing. In all her books she has so much to say, in addition to the story she is telling.

Theresa won the Carnegie Medal, one of the world's most prestigious prizes for children's literature, for *Whispers in the Graveyard*. Some journalists were disturbed by the story, and concerned that this award, judged by children's librarians, was honouring a book which was frightening, and dealt with terrible unhappiness. 'Let's get back to cosiness and fluffy bunnies,' one of them wrote. In her acceptance speech in 1995 Theresa responded to that criticism and

Whispers in the Graveyard

spoke of Beatrix Potter, the author and illustrator of *The Tale of Peter Rabbit*. Her books are still read nearly a century after they were first published.

'. . . Beatrix Potter did not fudge the telling of her story. Rabbits who wandered off into other people's gardens got put in pies. So there!'

Is the fact that she addressed real issues the reason her books are still around today? 'This is what I try to do in my writing, reflect reality, explore themes, deal with live issues. Young people are intelligent, articulate beings who are extremely aware of what is going on in the world. Yes, I am mindful of their vulnerability, the preciousness of childhood. I see this as the challenge for a modern-day writer of books for young children; to excite and thrill without traumatising, to expand imagination, make rainbows . . .'

Lindsey Fraser
1999

Bibliography
In date order

Simon's Challenge
Blackie 1988, Canongate 1989

When he loses his job, Simon's father leaves home to find work, leaving Simon bewildered and angry. Then he witnesses a theft and helps the local police in their enquiries. As he grapples with his family's problems with humour and common sense, forgotten pieces of the jigsaw begin to fall into place, along with a new sense of direction for his family.

Winner of the Kathleen Fidler Award 1988

Different Directions
Canongate 1989

Imagine being at the same school as your mother! Katharine is very embarrassed by the situation, especially the expectation that she will help her mother with her maths homework. She tries to make her mother's life a misery until she discovers something that makes her reassess the situation.

A Time to Reap
Blackie 1991

Arriving in Glasgow after many years in Europe, Anna has to adjust to a different climate, school and way of life. With kindness and support, she begins to enjoy her new life and finds the confidence to be herself. However, dark issues begin to emerge in her life which threaten her new-found happiness.

New School Blues
Canongate 1992

When she arrives at her new secondary school, Mary is immediately sure that she and Jamie, an obvious rebel, can be great friends. When they realise that a local right of way is going to be blocked by a farmer they embark on some in-depth archaeological research, take on the farmer and the authorities – and win!

Bullies at School
Canongate 1993

Siobhan is unhappy and lonely, the target of school bullies

and the butt of class jokes. Gradually, with the help of a sympathetic teacher and her discovery of Celtic myths and legends, she finds strength within herself to begin to deal with her problems.

Kezzie
Mammoth 1993

A story of great love, heroism and adventure in which a young girl leaves her west of Scotland home to look for her younger sister, Lucy. Kezzie makes the traumatic journey across the Atlantic to Canada where, with the help of the McMaths, she searches for her sister. She is tempted to stay but knows that their grandfather is awaiting their return to Scotland.

A Homecoming for Kezzie
Mammoth 1995

Kezzie and Lucy are reunited with their grandfather in Clydebank where they make a home in a tenement flat. Lucy settles well, but it is not until Kezzie finds work at the local Italian deli that she begins to settle down. Then come wave after wave of German bombers, and the community has to live from day to day, never knowing what they will wake up to find.

Whispers in the Graveyard
Mammoth 1994

Solomon's mother has left home, his father drinks heavily and his teachers have no patience with him. His only haven of peace and quiet is the local graveyard where he goes to be alone. The graveyard, however, is not all that it seems and gradually a force of evil begins to emerge, threatening to overwhelm him. It is only when he finds someone he can trust that he begins to see a way out of his predicament.

Winner of the Carnegie Medal 1994

Missing
Mammoth 1995 (first published under the name Maria Palmer) reprinted 1999

Andi and Liz are shopping in the very shopping mall from which a local teenager has recently disappeared. An astrological portrait seems the perfect Christmas gift – Andi is convinced that astrology is nonsense, so surely there would be no harm . . . She allows herself to be persuaded and so begins a whole new chain of frightening events.

Background: cover artwork by Maria Teresa Meloni for *Whispers in the Graveyard*

Alien Force
Dutton 1995

Jodie has been sent to Earth, disguised as a child in a children's home, to discover the ways of the planet and to transmit his discoveries, via his Calling Crystal, to his own planet. Eventually he realises that his true identity has been discovered and that his life is in danger. Time begins to run out for him . . .

Death or Glory Boys
Mammoth 1996

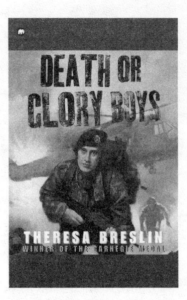

The aftermath of a terrorist bombing is terrible enough, but for four friends it throws up all sorts of questions about defence, the armed forces and legitimate force. Phil is against all forms of violence while Sarah sees the defence of the country as a responsibility to be shared by all. Their friendship is threatened by their difference of opinion and for the first time there are areas of their lives about which they can't talk freely. Meanwhile, the bomber plans the next attack . . .

Blair the Winner
Mammoth 1997

Four very funny stories about Blair, a middle child, and his family. Blair always thinks he is terribly hard done by, and he often is, but he is quite a character and, together with baby Willis, his big sister Melissa, Mum, Dad and Granny, there are fun and games wherever they go.

Name Games
Mammoth 1997

Jane loathes her name. She thinks her life would be far more exciting if it was more exotic. When she suggests to her parents that she wants to change her name, they are quite happy to go along with the idea, so she decides on

Scheherazade. Her decision affects her entire class – including the teacher – and before long everybody is name-swapping, with some confusing and very funny results.

Across the Roman Wall
A&C Black 1997

When Marinetta and Lucius first meet, the circumstances are far from auspicious and there seems little possibility of any friendship, let alone the strong bond which later develops and which saves their lives. Set in 397 AD, this is a fascinating and gripping adventure in which they find themselves transported far away from their homes and families in Roman Britain.

Bodyparts
A&C Black 1998

A graphic novel, illustrated by Janek Matysiak, about sabotage in a clinic exploring the possibility of cloning parts of the body for use in surgery. Shaun uncovers a plot to damage the clinic but can't work out who is responsible. The longer it takes to find out, the greater the danger he and his colleagues are in . . .

The Dream Master

Doubleday 1999

Despite great disapproval from the Dream Master, Cy discovers that he can return to interrupted dreams. In those dreams, he isn't the clumsy schoolboy he is in real time. He has more control – or at least he thinks he does. The Dream Master's greatest fears are realised when Cy returns to his time with an Egyptian prince, a situation that leads to all sorts of confusion and hilarity. But the pressure is on to return Aten to his own time – and his tomb . . .

Blair Makes a Splash

Mammoth 1999

Four more adventures with Blair, focusing on a holiday at the beach, a fishing trip from which the intrepid fisherman returns with a packet of frozen fish fingers, an embarrassing visit to the dentist and a clever solution to Blair's determination to have a tree house.

Starship Rescue

Barrington Stoke 1999

Marc is chosen to make the daring escape from the Fortress in this tense science fiction thriller written for a series of books specially created for those who find reading a challenge. So much depends on his agility and ability to remain hidden. He must make contact with the starship which makes its way from Earth only every twenty years.

Short Stories

Theresa Breslin has also written short stories that appear in the following collections.

Amazing Adventure Stories
Doubleday 1994

Dear Mum, Don't Panic
Mammoth 1995

Best of Friends
Mammoth 1995

Magic Carpet
Ginn 1995

All for Love
Mammoth 1997

A Braw Brew – Stories in Scots
Watergaw 1997

Just What I Always Wanted
Collins 1998

Turning Points
Hodder 1999

Centuries of Stories
HarperCollins 1999